snowy saplings

snowy saplings

peter waldor

SHANTI ARTS PUBLISHING

BRUNSWICK, MAINE

snowy saplings

Published by Shanti Arts Publishing

Designed by Shanti Arts Designs

Cover image: rvika/stock.adobe.com
Interior images: Vink Fan/stock.adobe.com

Shanti Arts LLC
193 Hillside Road
Brunswick, Maine 04011
shantiarts.com

Printed in the United States of America

ISBN: 978-1-956056-84-6 (softcover)

Library of Congress Control Number: 2023934848

for Eric Trommer

Books by Peter Waldor

Door to a Noisy Room

The Wilderness Poetry of Wu Xing

Who Touches Everything

The Unattended Harp

State of the Union

Gate Posts With No Gate

Nice Dumpling

Owl Gulch Elegies

Unmade Friend

Something About the Way

The Way 2

Midwife vs Obstetrician

Hats Off

Seven Quilts (essays)

Storytellers
only tell
of giant trees
From here
on they
won't stop
telling
tales of
saplings

Being
buried
alive
no
problem
for
this
sapling
Her
body
props
up
a
swell
in
the
hoarfrost
crown

Sapling
with
top hat
of snow
A
Time Square
mime
who won't
roll
her eyes
to the
spackle
pail of
tourist
dollars

Strange
winds
blew
a perfect
snow
cone
around
a sapling
Just one
hole
towards
the top
cue ball
sized
In that
hole
the small
top shoot
botanists
call the
apical
meristem
peers out

Peers out
like the
eye atop
the pyramid
blind and
seeing
across
universes
and back
through time
and ahead
through time
Don't expect
it to
listen

Not
enough
surface
to be
blown
down by
big winds
In fact
the sapling
barely
shivers
in death
blows

In filtered
sunlight
a sapling
rises
out of its
dropped
skirt
of snow
Stop
Marvel
at the
fresh
nakedness

Sapling
knocked
over at a
harsh angle
Needles
glowing
Almost
turquoise
Who knows
how many
scores
of years
it will
claw
for sun
from its
slanted
station

Old conifer
blown down
just a
serrated
yellow fin
where the
trunk
once was
Passing
bipeds
mourn
the loss
They don't
notice
the nearby
sapling
and bless
the child

Sapling
alone
outlier
a bit
above
tree line
We cover
our ears
or go deaf
from its
growing
pains and
pleasures

A krummholz
the size of
a sapling but
three hundred
years old
A sapling
the size of
a krummholz
but way
older

Sapling with
twelve small
cross branches
and the crown
plume crooked
Home to no
creatures yet
But passing
critters dream
of how
lucky their
grandchildren
will be
living in
that giant
future

Sapling
Fighting
for life
Fighting
for life
Fighting
for life
and yet
just
humming
like a
lathe motor
before
the woodworker
applies
his screeching
chisel

Our hearts
go out
to birds
fighting
for life
in winter
but not to
the sapling
who moves
much less
to stay
warm

People
count
so when
I lay
in sweet
snow
by a
sapling
just an
inch tall
sprig
I count
and recount
the needles

What's harder
going up or
going down
The answer
was always
obvious
but not
anymore
Saplings
along
the way
have not
changed
size in
my half
a century

At the
misfortune
of imposing
my imagination
I see
a wizard's
cloak
in the few
branches
and though
her head
is not
visible
I know
it's there
incanting

Not taller
than a
tall man's
knee
or short
one's thigh
so the
Christian
identifying
bipeds
won't harm
them with
saws and
hatchets
to celebrate
a day
I don't
fathom

Three
sequoia
saplings
dead by a
window
in a
mountain
cabin
Of course
they'd never
last outside
but the
hermit
dreamed of
nursing
them and
walking
back to
California
with them
poking
from his
satchel

Bole
wide as a
Buffalo
nickel
Branches
wide as
mercury
dimes

Don't
stoop
and tap
the crown
like a dog
rather
lay down
in the
snow
next to the
sapling
Don't be
alarmed
if you
sink

Sapling
planted
in the
pot
of
universe
Each
piece
of
soil
a
snow
flake
Each
snow
flake
a
piece
of
soil

Amazing
how a
giant tree
falls
in the
forest
with
no one
looking
or
listening
It's free
to bob
and weave
on descent
so it won't
crush the
saplings
at the
landing
site

The
hermit
dumps
the
dead
sequoia
saplings
No
sentimentality
just
sadness

An
upturned
bottle brush
that's never
cleaned
a bottle
Quiet
amidst
hooves
and boots
and gnats
and lethargic
winter
butterflies

Saplings
so individual
in youth
before
they age
to look
alike trees

Meadow
not meadow
for long for
it's full of
saplings
many shaped
arrow
hunchback
large rock
balancing
on small
rock
folding
up fan
arms up
in a heist
arms down
in obeisance
sketch idea
for drying
rack
asymmetrical
cellar
spider
goddess
with many
arms each
holding an
essential
instrument

Sapling
waiting
Sometimes
there is
an opening
in the canopy
sometimes not
and sometimes
there will be
and sometimes
there won't

The sapling
doesn't
have much
experience
with the
moon
It suspects
the snow
is landed
moonlight

The odds
of a
seed
germinating
The odds
of a
sapling
reaching
the top
of the
canopy
The odds
of the
canopy
not being
clobbered
Perfect
odds

Before
the
ultimate
differentiation
of parts
the green
needles
go up the
green trunk
as if it
were a
branch
These
are the
great days
before
the division
of labor
and
thickening
of skin

Passing
ungulate
speeding
but not
being
chased
kicks
a snow
clod off
a sapling
branch
and the
branch
snaps up
in fresh
liberty

Warm
winter day
Everywhere
branches
snapping
back
to form
out of
melting
snow

Saplings
listen to
the sound
of a distant
creek
never
stopped
by ice
They're like
children
alone
each in
their own
empty house
listening
to the
outside
with their
night
sharpened
ears
wondering
who will
open
the door

No thick
stench
from
old pine
cauldrons
The sapling
has just
a hint
of perfume

I know
someone
who
decades
before I
was born
chased
her son
around
their table
with a
rolling pin
in her
fist
Sapling
the size
of a
rolling
pin
Flour
sprinkles
off the pin
for she
was in
the middle
of baking

After
miles
walking
uncharted
forest
I stopped
and turned
back
I chose
a sapling
as a
marker
I'll head
for it
when I
return
trying
to go
deeper

The
Sapling
3/4s out
of a big
hand
of snow
like
a dove
being freed
from a
magician's
palm
Green
dove

In fact
the dove
and pine
are sister
cities
like Newark
New Jersey
and Oslo
In fact
the dove
pine and
magician
are sisters
In fact
the silk
scarf that
hides
all magic
is also
a sister

So many
shades
of green
So many
sizes
So many
degrees of
pointiness
Better
to call the
needles
wands
for they
don't stick
or thread
or even
prod
They
just
conjure

Whoomph
goes the
snow pack
compressing
an inch or few
along secret
fractures
and the
periscope
of the
sapling
capitulum
rises above
the delicate
combination
of crystals

White
seal pup
rests
on top
of a
sapling
which does
not strain
under the
great
relative
weight
Which
is out
of its

element
seal or
sapling
or even air
All elements
are out
of their
element
which is why
if any of us
have the
luxury
to relax
we feel
lost

The Sapling
is an
arrow
shooting
to the
center of
the earth
It's so fast
it looks like
it's not
moving
at all
The green
fletching
on the
capitulum
doesn't
even ruffle

Dead
sapling
The snow
falls through
the skeleton
which stops
nearly none
of the
crystals
All the many
angles and
turns of
the great
personality
are visible
along with
the nubs
that held
the green
needles now
brown and
woven into
the broad
loom

Saplings
fill up an
abandoned
mining road
People brush
snow off
stumps
alongside
to sit on
and watch
the little
ones
destroy
the old
way

When you
are quiet
imagine
the slow
winter sap
in the
sapling
circulatory
system

I have seen
mountain lions
three times
in my life
Mountain lions
have seen me
hundreds
of times
Same
idea with
saplings

Seed
factory
to seed
to seedling
to sapling
to something
monstrous
Graduation
after
graduation

Dimpled
Needled
Slender
bole
still
elastic
like a
fresh
rubber
band
just
snapped
onto a
rolled up
proclamation

Broken
milkweed
pappus
laid up on
a sapling
needle
It will
still
tumble
a few feet
despite
injuries

Two sprigs
make a
peace sign
limbs echoing
This youthful
intimacy
could
lead to
logistics
troubles
with light
and space
as adults

The sapling
fans out
above
and below
but of course
there is no
above and below
Directions
have
nothing
to do
with
saplings

All the
best spots
are left by
dead trees
Here a
sapling
setup on
a swell
left by
a *Picea*
engelmannii
that passed
away

Peter Waldor is the author of fourteen books of poetry and one book of essays. *Who Touches Everything* (Settlement House Press) won the National Jewish Book Award in 2014. *Gate Posts With No Gate* (Shanti Arts) was a mixed media collaboration with a group of artists. Waldor lives in Ophir, Colorado.

SHANTI ARTS

NATURE • ART • SPIRIT

Please visit us online
to browse our entire book catalog,
including poetry collections and fiction,
books on travel, nature, healing, art,
photography, and more.

Also take a look at our highly regarded art
and literary journal, *Still Point Arts Quarterly*,
which may be downloaded for free.

www.shantiarts.com

www.ingramcontent.com/pod-product-compliance
Lightning Source LLC
Chambersburg PA
CBHW051432270326
41934CB00019B/3487